You Play Like a Girl

Also By JoAnn Fastoff

White Sox (and other baseball worth mentioning) for Women

Two Years of Heaven: Rekindled Stories of Happiness

The Howard Watson mystery series
    The Scheduler
    The Standing People
    The Smoke Ring
    The Lie
    The Pact
    The Gordian Knot

You Play Like a Girl

JoAnn Fastoff

www.JoAnnFastoff.com

Table of Contents

"You play ball...like a girl!"

The Sandlot, 1993

Introduction

What does it mean to play like a girl? That boys who play like girls don't know how to play sports at all? Or that girls don't know how to play sports at all? Both statements are condescending.

"For many people," according to Joe McCarthy in *Global Citizen*, "Playing like a girl means being bad. Being too slow. Being clumsy. Being too weak. Striking out. Dropping a catch. Missing a tackle. Missing a shot. Getting crossed up."

It's easy for boys to play sports. Parents push them into it. Girls face challenges first from their parents, who never see them as athletes. They also face challenges from the many people who want to define their sexuality (usually incorrectly). And girls face challenges from the moment they step onto a field of play. They are mocked because they are female, and if they are girls of color, the bullying doesn't stop. Some male critics have written that athletics is "dangerous to feminine nature."

One day, Major League Baseball (MLB), National Hockey League (NHL), and National Football League (NFL) will allow women to play at the major league level, not just coach, although this is a tremendous start. Female athletes are undervalued in both money and advertising terms. Do the owners believe that money won't pour into the stadiums to watch women play? Yep. Their justification is that the men have larger audiences and more lucrative broadcast rights deals. (They also have history on their side, so this rhetoric is fecal matter.)

We have already seen the crowds rush to women's soccer, Ladies Professional Golf Association (LPGA), volleyball, tennis, and Women's National Basketball Association (WNBA) games. Millions of people attend women's tournaments, and millions watch their games on television, and the National Collegiate Athletic Association (NCAA) receives millions of dollars from advertisers. How do the owners conclude that women's games have no value? "Politics...the art of the possible."

According to Nielsen Women's Sports Research from 2018, "The rate of change in women's sports is one of the most exciting trends in the sports industry. The interest in women's sports is huge, and 84 percent of general sports fans have shared an interest in women's sports."

Of those general sports fans, 51 percent were male, confirming that half the fans were women interested in watching women's sports.

In 2013, ESPN, the Entertainment and Sports Programming Network cable TV program, noted men accounted for the majority of its WNBA audience...66 percent! Today's sports fans want athleticism, skill, and competition, no matter the gender. Playing like a girl means "ain't no downside."

The bullying didn't stop these women: Mary Lou Retton and Simone Biles, gymnastics; Billie Jean King, Martina Navratilova, and Serena Williams, tennis; Anne Meyers, Cheryl Miller, and Nancy Lieberman, basketball; Mickey Wright and Annika Sorenstam, golf; Laila Ali, boxing; Ronda Rousey, mixed-martial arts; Jackie Joyner-Kersee, Florence Griffith Joyner, and Allyson Felix, track and field; Misty May-Treanor and Kerri Walsh Jennings, American beach volleyball; Peggy Fleming, Dorothy Hamil, and Michelle Kwan, figure skating; Dara Torres, Katie Ledecky, and Simone Manuel, swimming; Mia Hamm and Abby Wambach, soccer; Lindsay Vonn, Alpine skiing; Ibithaj Muhammad, saber fencing; Danica Patrick, NASCAR; Ila Borders and Justine Siegel, baseball; Julie Krone, Cheryl White, and Rosie Napravnik, horse racing.

At this writing, the Miami Marlins named Kim Ng the first female General Manager of an MLB team, and Bianca Smith became the first Black female coach in the Boston Red Sox

Minor League. Not to be outdone, football took a bow when Sarah Fuller, who kicked off for Vanderbilt, became the first woman to play in a Power 5 football game, and Jennifer King became the first full-time Black female coach for the Washington Football Team.

A huge *however* is missing. The women mentioned above are incredible athletes and sports executives, but who led the charge? Who had to deal with being "first" or had to be ignored through their trials in the US, stemming from racism, sexism, and chauvinism? Who had to listen to the catchphrase of the day, "Girls should be home cooking and cleaning like their mothers." And who had to deal with the never-ending mantra that "Girls' programs should not be taking the money away from boys' sports budgets!"

The following women had to deal with it, that's who.

PART ONE: SWIMMING

The first decade of the twentieth century saw the women's fight for access to the water about to go down. A challenge facing women was what was considered "acceptable" clothing for women in public. Governing bodies like the Amateur Athletic Union (AAU) wanted women to be covered from "shoulder to toe" when they raced in public. United States women swimmers were left with very little choice but to create self-governing organizations like the National Women's Life-Saving League and later the Women's Swimming Association (WSA). High on the list of priorities was the right to wear bathing suits that didn't include stockings, a skirt, and shoes into the water!

In the same decade, Annette Kellerman, an

Australian, had created a new swimming look, a one-piece swimsuit that exposed the lower half of her legs. American women were instantly in love, and not surprisingly, it only took a few years for this suit to become the standard in the United States…with limits.

While women pushed for voting rights in the suffrage era, they also fought for equality in athletic activities, especially swimming. They believed that fighting for more equal clothing options would further help the fight of equality.

Gertrude Caroline "Trudy" Ederle was born on October 23, 1905, in New York City. She was the third of six children born to upper-middle-class German immigrants. Her father, Henry, who ran a butcher shop, taught her to swim in neighboring New Jersey, where the family owned a summer cottage. Even at age 12, Ederle loved swimming so much that she knew she would be an award-winning swimmer.

In the early days of competitive swimming, goggles were considered a piece of training equipment like fins, which meant they weren't permitted in swim meets. However, no rule said Ederle couldn't wear them swimming across the English Channel. To protect her eyes from saltwater, her sister, Margaret, sealed the motorcycle-type goggles with paraffin, making them watertight.

(Today, goggles are a multi-million-dollar accessory industry and virtually every swimmer dons a head cap and goggles in meets, all thanks to Hall of Famer David Wilkie who started the tradition.)

Most people had viewed this dream of Ederle's as foolishness because no woman had ever tried this "stunt" and only five men had been able to swim the English Channel before Ederle. The best time had been 16 hours, 33 minutes by Enrique Tirabocchi. Ederle's father promised her a red roadster if she could tackle the English Channel. What incentive for a teenager! Not only did she complete the swim to Kingsdown, England, she hit the beach in 14 hours and 34 minutes, two hours faster than any man before her. On August 6, 1926, Trudy Ederle became the first woman to swim across the English Channel at the age of 19. (Yep, she got the roadster!)

When Ederle returned home to the United States, she was greeted by near-riotous crowds and excited admirers who welcomed her at the New York dock. Mayor Jimmy Walker congratulated her, and President Calvin Coolidge, who called her "America's Best Girl," invited her to the White House. Her record remained unbroken until 1950. After suffering a severe back injury in 1933, she never competed again, although she did give swim performances at the 1939 New York World's Fair.

Ederle's achievement in swimming the English Channel made a lasting contribution to women's sports during a decade in which gender roles were shifting. As an American competitive swimmer, Olympic champion, and former world record-holder in five events, Ederle proved a woman could equal (or even eclipse) a man in one of the most physically demanding swims in the world. Albeit American aviator Charles Lindbergh went on to blot out her fame the next year (after flying solo and nonstop across the Atlantic Ocean), Ederle's astonishing accomplishment at the time set in place fantastic opportunities for women in athletics.

Ederle achieved a lifetime record of 29 US and world swimming records, and even today, the popular annual 17.5-mile swim from New York City's Battery Park to Sandy Hook, New Jersey, is named the Ederle Swim. Ederle was inducted into the **International Swimming Hall of Fame as an "Honor Swimmer" in 1965, and the National Women's Hall of Fame** in 2003. A recreation center, complete with a pool, bears her name on the Upper West Side of Manhattan, not far from where she grew up and first learned to swim.

Since childhood, Ederle had difficulty hearing due to a bout with measles. She further damaged her hearing during the English Channel swim, which caused her eventual deafness. After her competitive swimming days were over, Ederle enjoyed a successful career helping to create breakthrough techniques for swimmers with hearing impairments, including teaching swimming to children at the Lexington School for the Deaf. Ederle never married and died in 2003 of natural causes at the tender age of 98 in Wyckoff, New Jersey.

PART TWO: GOLF

A lot of people believe that the word "golf" originated from the acronym "Gentlemen Only Ladies Forbidden." It didn't—just seems that way. Women these days probably take as many trips around the links as their male equivalents, and golf has grown to be a pastime enjoyed by both sexes. In golf, the underlying principle of the rules is fairness, as stated on the back cover of the official rule book:

- Play the ball as it lies.
- Play the course as you find it.
- If you cannot do either, do what is fair.

Seems fairness has not gained *any* footing based on the idea of women playing the game alongside men. Although women, in general, can't hit their shots as far as men, elite women golfers are about as skilled as male pros at approach shots, chips, and putts.

Sexual discrimination is still rampant in the world of golf. And women's golf suffers more because of this wound than any other female sports. The only reason for the establishment of the LPGA, et al., is because men denied women admission to many golf clubs for decades.

After all, "Golf is the very essence of male comradeship, manly, virile, and the modern substitute for the swashbuckling red-blooded (masculinity) of all human endeavors" (Anonymous).

What woman could compete with that? What woman would want to?

The heckling and implications of lesbianism cut the deepest. Men don't want women playing in men's golf tournaments but don't want women playing in their own league either. And men diminish women's golf even more because no matter what the women players accomplish, men still seem to say, "So what?"

Mildred "Babe" Didrikson Zaharias will probably go down in sports history as one of the greatest female athletes of all time. The woman could do it all—and do it well. If she touched a golf club, tennis racket, running shoes, discus, javelin, or basketball, all other competitors could forget any chances of coming in first.

Born in Port Arthur, Texas in 1911, Didrikson was the sixth of seven children born to new Americans from Norway. When Didrikson turned four years old, the family moved 23 miles north to Beaumont. In the 1920s, the Ku Klux Klan controlled local politics in Beaumont, which had become a primary form of opposition to Reconstruction and pledged to support the supremacy of the white race. The success of D. W. Griffith's film *Birth of a Nation,* based on the book *The Clansman,* in 1915, had helped fan the flames of racial hatred. This is the climate to which Babe Didrikson was allowed to flourish.

Sportswriters in the first half of the twentieth century typified the attitude toward women athletes. Some even went as far as to say, "It would be much better if (Didrikson) and her ilk stayed home, got themselves prettied up and waited for the phone to ring." Since women were not encouraged to compete in sports at this time, Didrikson faced a lot of sexism, starting with claims that she might not be a woman because she was physically strong, and criticized for it.

Some in the sports circle believed Didrikson married wrestler George Zaharias to erase all suspicion that she wasn't a woman. It must have been tough being reminded often that she was not an attractive woman. It must have been even tougher taking physical exams (too often) to prove she *was* a woman. On top of this, it must have been painful to hide the fact that she was a lesbian, something in the men's sports world, and the state of Texas, would have never condoned.

In 1950, Didrikson helped found the LPGA when she revolutionized the sport. She was America's first female golf celebrity, clearing a path for Mickey Wright and Annika Sorenstam some sixty years later. Didrikson is recognized as the world record holder for the farthest baseball thrown by a woman and the only track and field athlete (male or female) to win individual Olympic medals in the running, throwing, and jumping events. Her credentials are larger than life:

- 1951 LPGA Hall of Fame
- 1957 Bob Jones Award (the highest honor given by USGA for Distinguished Sportsmanship)
- 1976 National Women's Hall of Fame
- 2008 Colorado Women's Hall of Fame.

In 2000, *Sports Illustrated Magazine* named Didrikson on its list of the greatest female athletes of all time behind Jackie Joyner-Kersee. She was also named the Tenth Greatest North American Athlete of the twentieth century by ESPN, and the Ninth Greatest Athlete of the twentieth century by the Associated Press.

Babe Didrikson Zaharias died of colon cancer at the age of 45 in 1956.

Nancy Marie Lopez was born on January 6, 1957, in Torrance, California, to Mexican-American parents. Lopez's father, Domingo, an avid golfer and the owner of an auto-body repair shop, introduced her to the game of golf at age eight, and gave Nancy her first set of golf clubs while guiding her development. Although born in California, Lopez grew up in New Mexico, where she won the New Mexico Women's Amateur at age 12. Then she won the US Junior Girls Amateur Championship in 1972 and 1974. Her high school did not have a girls' golf team, so she played on the boys' team and helped them win two state championships.

But the pressure of competition took its toll. "I was so scared I always threw up," she admitted to *Sports Illustrated* magazine. "I carried a trash can with me. My dad told me,

'If you're going to play golf, you've got to get over being sick.' I didn't want to quit, so I decided to get over it." She did get over it; the winning continued. Lopez tied for second in the US Women's Open as a 17-year-old amateur in 1975.

Lopez's father, who had a third-grade education, would not let her work. He wouldn't even allow her to do the dishes. "No, Mama," he would tell Nancy's mother. "These hands are meant for golf."

For five years, Lopez wore braces her family could not afford. Her father always believed she would be famous as he brought her up to be a champion; her mother, Marina, brought her up to be a lady. Lopez was raised as royalty, the countess of golf, and she was just 21. And of course, racial discrimination left its stain. Because the Lopez family was of Mexican descent, Lopez's parents were not allowed to join the Country Club of Roswell near their home, so Nancy had to play in Albuquerque, 200 miles away.

Twentieth century golf needed a popular champion for everyone to embrace. Nancy Lopez was good-looking, busty, with dark brown eyes and hair, and equipped with a smile that reflected her joy...and she was heterosexual. Mickey Wright, probably the most significant female golfer of the modern era, was amazed at her composure. "Never in my life have I seen such control in someone so young," she said.

Although Lopez's career was pretty much an instant success, her mother died from a heart attack before ever seeing Lopez win a professional tournament. Lopez's father encouraged her to stay the course despite this tragedy.

From the late 1970s to the late 1980s, Nancy Lopez was the game's best player, winning three majors at the LPGA Championship. At the University of Tulsa, Lopez was named a 1976 All-American and the university's Female Athlete of the Year. She never won the US Women's Open but finished second four times. She is also the only player to win the Rookie of the Year Award, Player of the Year Award, and **Vare Trophy** in the same season (1978). By the time she was 30, Lopez had won enough tournaments, 35, to qualify for the LPGA Hall of Fame. Most golf historians rank Lopez among the five best LPGA players of all time. She was inducted into the **World Golf Hall of Fame in** 1987.

Nancy Lopez gave birth to three daughters with her second husband, Ray Knight, before hanging up her clubs in 2002. She emerged again in 2007 but was never able to make the cuts in significant events. She has a line of clothing and equipment for women golfers, called Nancy Lopez Golf. She currently resides in Florida, where she hosts an annual golf tournament to benefit the charity AIM (Adventures in Movement), which helps mentally challenged, visually impaired, hearing impaired, physically disabled, and other children and adults with special needs.

PART THREE: TRACK & FIELD

According to Wikipedia, the name "track and field" is derived from where the sport takes place, a running track and a grass field for throwing and some of the jumping events. Track and field are categorized under the umbrella sport of athletics, including road running, cross country running, and race walking. And, because running, jumping, and throwing are natural forms of human physical expression, track and field-style events are among the oldest of all sporting competitions. In ancient times, track and field were held in conjunction with festivals and sports meets, like the Olympic Games held initially in Greece.

It didn't take a lot for colleges to ignore the constraints placed on women athletes in the last vestiges of the nineteenth century. However, Vassar College decided to drown out all the noise and held its first-ever women's field day in 1895, featuring competition in five track and field events. Soon colleges across the country were offering women the opportunity to compete.

Up until the early 1920s, track and field had been almost exclusively a male-only pursuit. Although many women, but mainly Alice Milliat, argued for women's inclusion at the Olympics, the International Olympic Committee refused. So, what did Milliat do? She founded the International Women's Sports Federation in 1921.

Alongside a growing women's sports movement in Europe and North America, and working in conjunction with the English Women's Amateur Athletic Association (WAAA), the Women's World Games were held four times between 1922 and 1934. These events ultimately led to introducing five track and field events for women in the 1928 Summer Olympics. (In China, women's track and field events were also being held in the 1920s, but were subject to criticism and disrespect from audiences.) From 1922 to 1960, thousands of women competed and won many gold medals with little encouragement or recognition (read: endorsements). Wilma Rudolph's triumphant Olympics in 1960 sparked renewed support for women's track and field in the United States.

In 1972, Title IX began to create a genuinely level playing field for men and women. Its purpose was to prohibit sex or gender discrimination in all educational activities or programs that received federal funds...especially athletics. In 2021, more women than men represented Team USA at the 2021 Tokyo Olympics. Of the 613 athletes competing for Team USA this summer, 329 were women and 284 were men. This marked the third straight Olympic Games with more women on the roster, officials have said. And because of more access to opportunity, women were able to begin bridging the gaps that had been in place between men and women for generations before.

Prior to 1972, fewer than 4 percent of girls played high school sports at a varsity level. About three million teenage girls (42.7 percent) are playing at the high school level today because of Title IX. Teen girls are still not receiving true equal access, even if the school is following the letter of the law, but many girls exhibit more self-confidence and are more outgoing because they've had equal access to opportunities compared to men.

Title IX did not exist at the time for the following women in track and field. They did not reach the Olympics with the help of corporate sponsorship money or uplifting support from the country they were representing, but from talent, unwavering courage, perseverance, and encouragement from family and friends.

Neither Buckingham Fountain nor Soldier Field existed in 1914 Chicago. Automobiles and cable cars outnumbered horse-drawn carriages on the street and unfortunately traffic lights did not come on the scene for at least another decade. The largest immigrant group was the Germans and try as they might, they could not keep the US neutral in World War I. The war shut off immigration and siphoned native-born labor into the war effort. Many Chicago employers turned to women and African Americans, hiring them for jobs previously reserved for white men.

These new opportunities, mainly in heavy industry, stimulated the Great Migration of African Americans from the South to Chicago and other northern cities. At the same time that Black people moved from the South, Chicago was still receiving thousands of immigrants from southern and eastern Europe. Not surprisingly, the groups clashed with each other for jobs.

Women weren't even an afterthought in Chicago politics. Neither Democrats nor Republicans made any serious approaches to securing women's party loyalty, especially since they couldn't vote. So, they remained primarily excluded from Chicago politics. Ironic that the women's suffrage agendas during this time acquiesced to southern white women, so "their" suffrage did not include any allegiance to Black women. This is the Chicago to which **Theodora Ann "Tidye" Pickett** was born.

Pickett could run, and run well, and eventually her athletic ability caught the attention of John Brooks, a University of Chicago long jumper, who was headed to the Olympics, and who became her mentor and coach. "[John Brooks] made sure I had my first pair of good running shoes," Pickett said. The *Chicago Defender* newspaper called her the "Ace dash star on the board of education playgrounds track team."

Almost one thousand miles to the east of Chicago sits the city of Malden, Massachusetts, a southern suburb of Boston. Malden is the home of many notable people including actor Walter Brennan, writer Erle Stanley Gardner, The Ames Brothers singing quartet and, in 1913, welcomed the birth of **Louise Stokes,** future Olympic competitor and founder of the Colored Women's Bowling League.

Tidye Pickett and Louise Stokes became the first African-American women to ever be invited to the Olympic Games held in Los Angeles in 1932. Pickett was named to the American Olympic Team as part of the eight-woman 4x100 meter relay pool.

The women might have been invited to the Games but that was about it. Due to what most people believe was racism, Pickett and Stokes were bumped from the final four-woman relay lineup at the last minute by the coach, George Vreeland, who replaced them with two white runners.

"Babe" Didrikson, the US darling of the 1932 Olympics, made no secret of how much she detested the Black women's presence and felt they should not be on the team. She went as far as dousing them both with cold water while they slept on the train to Los Angeles. She wanted them to go back to where they came from. Pickett and Stokes came from generations born in America. Didrikson was first generation American from Norway.

Pickett and Stokes were not permitted to eat or sleep with their team and were not invited to do media appearances or attend the banquet in the hotel ballroom. Although the NAACP sent a telegram urging that the Black runners be treated fairly, the group received no response from the US Olympic Committee. Both women were included in the picture taken of the US Field and Track team, but both women watched from the bench the other US Women receive gold medals.

Being replaced at the last minute caused Pickett and Stokes to return home, feeling humiliated and having nothing to show for having been on an Olympic team. Although Stokes was the recipient of many track and field awards prior to the Olympics, her invisibility at the 1932 and 1936 Olympics would make most people believe otherwise.

In the 1936 Olympics in Berlin, Pickett and Stokes qualified again for the Olympics. Both said they felt less threatened by Adolph Hitler's agenda toward them than the racism they had to endure from their US coaches and teammates. Malden was a small but vibrant African American community that encouraged Stokes and even raised the necessary funds to send her to Berlin in 1936, but Stokes did not qualify in her heat and Pickett broke her foot while running hurdles. Both women watched the rest of the Olympics from the bench.

Louise Stokes returned to her hometown in Malden to a hero's parade. She remained active and started the Colored Women's Bowling League, winning many titles. In addition, she was honored by the Massachusetts Hall of Black Achievement and has a statue in the Malden High School courtyard.

Tidye Pickett later received her bachelor's and master's degree in education and became a school teacher. She retired as a principal in 1980. Her school, which is now gone, was renamed for her.

Many won't recognize her name but many will recognize her significance in sports. In 1948, **Alice Coachman** was the first Black woman to ever win an Olympic gold medal when she won the high jump competition.

Born in Albany, Georgia in 1923, Coachman was the recipient of racism at its deepest level—Jim Crow. Because she was not allowed to train at facilities or participate in organized sports due to her color, she had to train on what was available to her. The double whammy was that she was female. She loved jumping and she ran shoeless along the dirt roads near her home, using homemade equipment to practice her jumping.

Despite the reservation of her parents (because she was a girl), Coachman started running track in high school. At age 16 she was offered a scholarship to the Tuskegee Preparatory School. The scholarship required her to work while studying and training, which included cleaning and maintaining sports facilities as well as mending uniforms.

Coachman dominated AAU women's high jump championships from 1939 through 1948. Although she won ten championships in a row, she would not be able to compete in the 1940 or 1944 Olympics because they were canceled due to World War II.

Coachman will always be a "what if the Olympics had not been canceled?" athlete, because many in the sports field believe she would have gone on to be the number one female athlete of all time. In the high jump finals of the 1948 Summer Olympics in London, Coachman leaped 5 feet, 6⅛ inches on her first try and won the Gold.

Coachman returned home to the US, a hero. Although she received honors from England's King George VI, President Harry S. Truman, and First Lady Eleanor Roosevelt, the mayor of her town in Georgia refused to shake her hand.

In 1952, Alice Coachman became the first Black woman to endorse an international product, namely Coca Cola. In her hometown, a street and an elementary school were named in her honor. She was inducted into the USA Track and Field Hall of Fame in 1975, the Georgia Sports Hall of Fame in 1979, and the United States Olympic Hall of Fame in 2004. Without a doubt, she paved the athletic way for the likes of Evelyn Ashford and Allyson Felix.

Alice Coachman died at the age of 90 in Albany, Georgia on July 14, 2014.

Sixty years before Colin Kaepernick took a knee, **Eroseanna "Rose" Robinson** had already suffered the slings and arrows of outrageous racism in the US.

Rose Robinson was born in 1925 in Chicago. She was the second of three daughters born to a working-class family who lived on the city's South Side. In 1943, Rose, along with her sisters Adrienne and Bernice, led their area park (division) to the Central AAU track title. They earned four gold medals and two silvers between them, including the 4x100 meter relay, where the sisters made up three-fourths of the team.

In 1958, at the age of 33, Robinson qualified for, but declined to attend, the Moscow Games in Russia because she refused to be a political pawn or symbolic "ambassador of goodwill" on behalf of the United States, which she believed treated Black people like second-rate citizens.

In 1959, at the Pan American Games in Chicago, Robinson did something considered daring to everyone but herself—she sat out the National Anthem because she felt it did not represent Black people in their quest for equality. She believed Black people, especially women, could represent America outside of the US, sure, especially to promote the idea of racial harmony in the United States, but inside the US, America did not represent Black people on any level.

"Black women athletes have, and continue to take a great risk," she said, "in advocating for social and political change inside and outside of sports, even as they garner less visibility for their actions."

For Rose Robinson, sports gave her a sense of focus, drive, and confidence. All skills that she took with her to her job as a social worker and her steadfast involvement in the Civil Rights Movement.

In 1940, **Wilma Glodean "Skeeter" Rudolph** was born prematurely as the 20th of 22 children to a twice-married father in Clarksville, Tennessee. Rudolph's legacy lies in her efforts to overcome obstacles that included childhood illnesses and physical disability to become the fastest woman runner in the world in 1960.

After contracting scarlet fever and double pneumonia before she was six years old, Rudolph later lost strength in her left leg and foot due to a bout with polio. Physically disabled for much of her early life, Rudolph wore a leg brace until she was 12 years old. For two years, Rudolph and her mother made the weekly 50-mile bus trips to Nashville for treatments to regain the use of her very weak leg. She also received at-home massage treatments four times a day from family members and wore an orthopedic shoe for support of her foot for another two years. Rudolph was determined to erase the disability even though the odds were stacked against her from the start. "My doctors told me I would never walk again," she would repeat often. "My mother told me I would. I believed my mother." Rudolph credits her family as being instrumental in her rehabilitation.

In 1956 at age 16, Rudolph, Mae Faggs, Lucinda Williams, and Isabelle Daniels from Tennessee A & I State College brought home bronze medals in track from the Olympics in Melbourne, Australia. In 1960, at the Rome Olympics, Rudolph became the first American woman to win three gold medals in track and field at a single Olympics and was one of the primary role models for Black and female athletes. Many sports figures believe her Olympic success "gave a tremendous boost to women's track in the United States." In addition, Rudolph broke through gender barriers at previously all-male track and field events. She not only went on to break records but became an inspiration and changed the history of track and field.

Wilma Rudolph succumbed to brain and throat cancer at age 54 in 1994.

Prior to the emergence of Carl Lewis, Gail Devers, Shelly-Ann Fraser-Pryce, or Usain Bolt, there existed the woman who originally ran against the wind. She was the first person ever to win back-to-back track and field medals at the 1964 and 1968 Olympics.

Wyomia Tyus was born in Griffin, Georgia in 1945 to tenant dairy farmers in one of the few communities in Georgia that didn't lynch every young Black man falsely accused of rape by a white woman. She grew up in a primarily white neighborhood and became aware of her race and racial segregation at an early age.

Although a public school was within walking distance, it was an "all-white" school, so Tyus was forced to take an hour bus ride to a school for Blacks each day. The nearest Black family lived almost a mile away, so Tyus spent most of her time playing sports with her brothers and the white boys in the neighborhood. Her dairy-farmer father, Willie Tyus, helped to solidify the idea that she could accomplish anything in her life, but not without hard work. He also encouraged her, the only daughter of six kids, to compete in sports. Tyus' mother, Marie, however, felt engagement in sports was unladylike.

Tyus shrugged off her mother's objections and began playing basketball and soon enjoyed the competition so much that she decided to try the high jump for the track and field team. Though she struggled at the high jump, she realized she had a natural talent for running.

After finishing high school, Tyus attended Tennessee State University (TSU), making her the first of her family to go to college. She began training with TSU coach Ed Temple; however, a general lack of interest in her classes nearly made her become her own worst enemy, further obstructing her chances to compete in the 1964 Olympics.

Tyus's father died when she was a teenager, and Temple's influence and enduring presence in her life filled the shoes of the father-figure she needed. As Tyus often said, "Coach Temple was a visionary, doing for Black women what nobody else was even thinking of doing when Black women were seen as less than second-class citizens. His program produced 40 Olympic athletes and 27 medalists, which led to a 99 percent graduation rate. Education was as important as athletics to [Coach] Temple."

Temple helped her develop her focus, highlighting the struggle that comes with being a Black athlete and a female, and having to work harder to receive positive recognition.

Tyus did not miss his point. With three golds and one silver medal, Wyomia Tyus of Tennessee State was the most successful of all US women track and field athletes at the Olympics. She also holds the distinction of being the first athlete (male or female) to defend an Olympic 100-meter title successfully. She won the 100-meter title in 1964 with a new world record of 11.2 and, in July 1965, brought the record down to 11.1, having two weeks earlier claimed a share of the 100-yard record. She also snagged the AAU Indoor 60-yard title three times and was the 200-meter champion at the 1967 Pan American Games. In 1968 she won the Olympic 100-meter, again setting a world record (11.0).

Tyus faced an atmosphere of racial tension during the Mexico City games in 1968, and African-American athletes (men) threatened to boycott the games. (Two sprinters, gold medalist Tommie Smith and bronze medalist John Carlos, were suspended from the US team for raising a Black Power salute during their victory ceremony.) Tyus won gold in the 100-meter dash for a second consecutive time, something no one else did until Carl Lewis competed 20 years later. In response to the suspension of her fellow athletes, Tyus's 400-meter relay team, which won the gold medal and set a new record, dedicated their medals to Smith and Carlos.

Wyomia Tyus married and had two sons. She became track and field coach at Beverly Hills High School and later capitalized on her celebrity by serving as a goodwill ambassador to Africa. She is the author of *Tigerbelle*, her memoir, co-written with Elizabeth Terzakis.

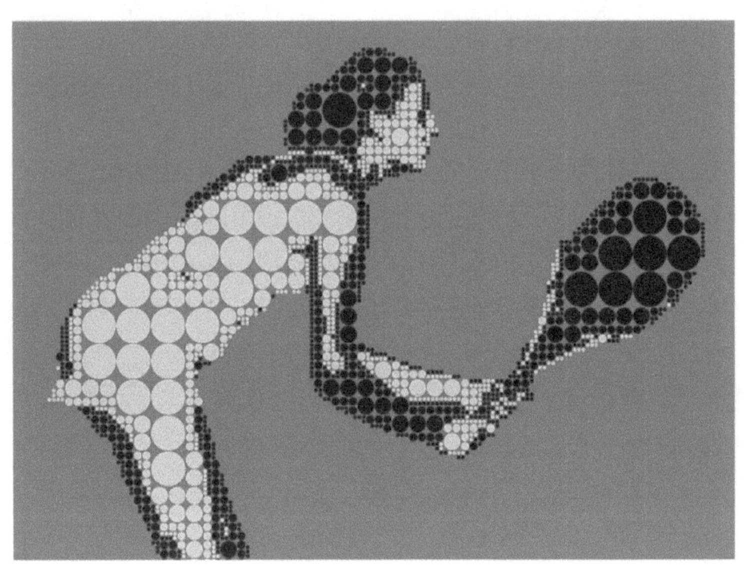

PART FOUR: TENNIS

When Billie Jean King beat Bobby Riggs at the "battle of the sexes" tennis tournament in 1973, she said later, "I thought it would set [women] back 50 years if I didn't win that match. It would ruin the women's tour and affect all women's self-esteem." She believed that she had destiny on her side to work for sexual equality in sports. However, King's biggest fear at the time was her sexuality getting out. When it finally emerged, after many years of denying the allegations, she eventually became the advocate for the LGBTQ+ community that she is today.

Even in athletics today, men and women are forced to maintain a particular image of heterosexuality. Those who are openly gay are still sometimes ashamed of this aspect of their life in their sport. Billie Jean King spoke out against this behavior and continues today. She remains an inspiration to all women, both gay and straight, in tennis and other sports.

Billie Jean was part of the "Original 9," a group of nine women athletes that formed the **Virginia Slims** Series because the women wanted to end the inequality of pay between male and female winners. These nine women created their tournaments and played wherever they could. Eventually, this turned into the **Women's Tennis Association (WTA)**.

May Sutton Bundy was born on September 25, 1886, in Plymouth, England, the youngest of seven children born to Adolphus Sutton, a retired British Navy captain, and Adeline Esther Godfrey. When she was six years old, Sutton's family moved to the US to a ranch near Pasadena, California. It was there that she and her sisters played tennis on a court built by her father and other English neighbors.

In 1903, at age 17, Sutton won the singles title at the US National Championships and in 1905 she became the first American player to win the singles title at Wimbledon. Sutton became the first American and first non-British woman to win the Wimbledon singles title when she beat British star and reigning two-time Wimbledon champion Dorothea Douglass Chambers in the challenge round. She did it while shocking the British audience by rolling up her sleeves to bare her elbows and wearing a skirt that showed her ankles. God bless teenagers.

At age 26, she married Tom Bundy, a three-time men's doubles title winner at the US Championships. She then semi-retired to raise their four children. However, in 1921 at the age of 35, she made a comeback and became the fourth-ranked player in the US. Four years later, she was a women's doubles finalist at the US Championships, and, although almost 40 years of age, she still qualified for America's **Wightman Cup** team, an annual team tennis competition for women between the US and Great Britain from 1923 through 1989. It was suspended in 1990 because, to be truthful, the US women dominated the contests, 55-10.

In the 1950s, Sutton Bundy became the first woman inducted into the US Lawn Tennis Association's Hall of Fame. In 1956, she was inducted into the International Tennis Hall of Fame. She never stopped playing tennis and was playing well into her late 80s. She died of cancer at age 89 in October, 1975 in Santa Monica, California.

When racism and sexism were much more unrestrained in sports and society, **Althea Neale Gibson** was often compared to baseball great Jackie Robinson. "Her road to success was a challenging one," said tennis trailblazer Billie Jean King, "but I never saw her back down." Tennis phenom Venus Williams wrote, "I am honored to have followed in such great footsteps (of Gibson). Her accomplishments set the stage for my (and my sister's) success…"

Althea Gibson was born in 1927 in Silver, South Carolina, to Daniel and Annie Bell Gibson, who worked as sharecroppers on a cotton farm. The Great Depression hit her family's and other farmers' pockets sooner than people in the cities. In 1930 the family packed up and moved to Harlem, a neighborhood in New York City, because they were told that jobs were plentiful.

The Harlem Renaissance was an intellectual, social, and artistic explosion centered in Harlem, New York City, during the 1920s. It was known as the "New Negro Movement," named after a 1925 anthology edited by Alain Locke. The movement was affected by The Great Migration of Black people from the South to the North, where job openings were in great demand. New York's Harlem was the largest group of Migration recipients in the US.

Gibson's family's life at this time had its hardships. The Great Depression caught up with the cities by this time, and her parents (now saddled with four children), struggled to make ends meet, even living on public assistance for a time. The younger Gibson was living a different kind of struggle, the one in the classroom, often skipping school altogether.

What Gibson didn't struggle in were sports. At first, basketball was her favorite. Next, she became quite proficient in paddle tennis. Gibson became so skilled in paddle tennis, that by 1939, at the age of 12, she was the New York City women's paddle tennis champion. Gibson quit school at the age of 13 and, terrified of her father's violent behavior, especially after dropping out of school, she ran away from home. She then spent time living in a Roman Catholic protective shelter for abused children. After a while, Gibson became a ward of the city and was given a small rent stipend to live on her own.

After a musician friend gave her a used tennis racquet as a gift, Gibson grasped quickly the idea that tennis was her way out of her turbulent life. With no means of financial, and especially, emotional support, she was forced to take menial jobs to make ends meet but continued with her athletic training, and in 1942 at the age of 15, she won the first tennis tournament she entered. The New York Junior Women's title was granted by the American Tennis Association (ATA), an organization for Black players. At the time, the United States Lawn Tennis Association (USTA) had no people of color as members.

In 1950, when Gibson was 23 years old, and after several years of receiving no invitations, several white players petitioned the USTA on her behalf and she was finally permitted to play at the US Nationals, becoming the first Black person to compete in the tournament. She didn't win but she didn't stop there. In 1956, Gibson became the first African American to win the French Championships Grand Slam title. The following year she won both Wimbledon and the US Nationals (later called the US Open). Just so no one thought she was a fluke, she won both Wimbledon and US Nationals again in 1958. She was voted Female Athlete of the Year by the Associated Press in both years.

The 5-foot-11 right-hander had what was deemed a "mannish" serve and good speed, which allowed her to quickly cover the court. As the years went on, she became more consistent from the baseline. She then went on to win 11 Grand Slam tournaments, five singles titles, five doubles titles, and one mixed doubles title. In 2018, the USTA unanimously voted to erect a statue honoring Gibson at Flushing Meadows, the US Open site. The statue, created by sculptor Eric Goulder and unveiled in 2019, is only the second Flushing Meadows monument erected in honor of an athlete. (Arthur Ashe is the other.)

Gibson was married twice but had no children from either union. She suffered strokes in her later years and was rarely seen in public after 1990. On September 28, 2003, Gibson died at the age of 76 in an East Orange, New Jersey hospital following treatment for an infection and a respiratory ailment. She is survived by a brother and a sister, and the Foundation bearing her name that she helped establish that provides athletic and educational opportunities to urban youth. Her awards are numerous.

She was inducted into the International Tennis Hall of Fame and the International Women's Sports Hall of Fame. In 1980 she became one of the first six inductees into the International Women's Sports Hall of Fame. Other inductions included the National Lawn Tennis Hall of Fame, the International Tennis Hall of Fame, the Florida Sports Hall of Fame, the Black Athletes Hall of Fame, the Sports Hall of Fame of New Jersey, the New Jersey Hall of Fame, the International Scholar-Athlete Hall of Fame, and the National Women's Hall of Fame. In 1988, Gibson received a Candace Award from the National Coalition of 100 Black Women.

Tennis great Martina Navratilova once commented that "[Gibson] was a great champion and a great person. We had a good relationship...she was always there for me even when I was a nobody."

When Gibson began playing tennis, fewer than 5 percent of tennis players were people of color. Today, over 30 percent are people of color, and two-thirds are African American. This increase in tennis playing among people of color is all due to Althea Gibson, who "always wanted to be somebody."

PART FIVE: RACE CAR DRIVING

To outrun the law, bootleggers (men running moonshine, rum, and whiskey during Prohibition-era 1920-1933) learned to "stock" and engineer their cars so efficiently that their car engines ran faster and handled better than any police vehicles chasing them. Some tire companies even assisted these so-called "runners" in producing top-quality tires for this maneuver. Bootlegging might have started as backwoods "racing from the law," but it quickly went beyond backwoods racing because of the numerous murderous roads and cliffs the driver had to travel through to get the product to the buyer.

What to do with all those "stocked" cars

once Prohibition ended? In 1936, the city of Daytona, Florida held the first organized stock car race as a promotion. It didn't make any money, but a Prohibition-era mechanic named Bill France was determined to find a way to make a buck from what he thought would take the car world by storm—stock car racing. Unfortunately, the storm lasted longer than he wanted. Eleven years later, the National Association for Stock Car Auto Racing (NASCAR) organized, formally announcing the sport in 1947.

The first NASCAR race was in Daytona on February 15, 1948. In a modified Ford, the winner was Red Byron, a former moonshine runner (of course). During its 72-year history, the NASCAR series has been mostly stripped of minority drivers. One driver, Bubba Wallace, is the lone Black driver, at this writing, who just became the first Black driver to win NASCAR in 58 years. Basketball phenom Michael Jordan heads up his racing team. Also, at this writing, Grammy-award winning artist Pit Bull heads up a NASCAR racing team. In recent years, NASCAR has acknowledged the subject of racism and has taken steps to further opportunities for people of color, but...not so much for women.

Sara Williams Christian was born on August 25, 1918, in Dahlonega, Georgia only two months before the Spanish Flu outbreak ravaged the world. The flu, which came in multiple waves from 1918-1919, killed more than 675,000 people in the US. Williams was born to outlive this.

She married Frank Christian, who was not only a businessman but also a former bootlegger. Frank knew how to drive a car, became very involved in racing, and used some of his profits from the moonshine business to purchase stock cars in the 1940s.

Sara later came to race some of these cars and made a name for herself by being one of the few women to compete during NASCAR's early years. She participated in races because of her husband. It was his love of racing that contributed to Sara's interest in the sport. Frank helped sponsor some of the best drivers in NASCAR during the 1940s and 1950s. His connection to well-known drivers in 1948 was when he, Charlie Mobley, and Bob Flock built New Atlanta Speedway in Morrow, Georgia, and invited Sara, her sister Mildred, and Ethel Flock Mobley to race there. They hoped the powder puff races would attract crowds.

It was the first time Christian had ever raced. When she won, she was so excited by the win that she started competing. Frank supported her in her races the following two years. The couple even competed against each other at Daytona in 1949, becoming the only husband and wife in NASCAR history. Frank finished the race in sixth place and Sara in eighteenth.

Christian competed in NASCAR's first strictly stock race at Charlotte Speedway in Charlotte, North Carolina on June 19, 1949. She finished 14th out of 33 drivers and was the only woman to participate, thereby becoming the first female to drive in a race promoted by NASCAR.

Soon, Sara Christian became the owner of several firsts: the first woman to drive in a NASCAR race; the first woman to record a top-five finish in NASCAR at the Heidelberg Raceway in Pittsburgh, Pennsylvania, and the first husband and wife to compete in the same NASCAR race. When Christian finished fifth at the Heidelberg Raceway in Pittsburgh, the finish was the best and only Top 5 finish by a woman in NASCAR history until Danica Patrick finally eclipsed it in 2011.

Christian opened the door for future women drivers like Janet Guthrie, Sarah Fisher, and Danica Patrick. Although she competed for only a year, she received the 1949 United States Drivers Association Woman Driver of the Year award. She was inducted into the Georgia Automobile Racing Hall of Fame in 2004.

Sara and Frank Christian had two children. She numbered her Ford 7/11 because it represented the ages of her children when she was racing. When she retired from racing in the early 1950s, the family moved to a town near Atlanta. She and Frank spent their days farming and operated the Cherokee Motel located in the area. She died in 1980 at age 61.

"It's idiotic." "Women racers a joke." "She oughta be home having babies...if she can." "Get the (breasts) out of the pits." "Incompetent." "Bitch."

Not-so-nice terms spit out by your "gentlemen" colleagues, but **Janet Guthrie** would make them eat their words as car racing is one of the few sports where men and women compete with each other on the same field at the same time. After the driver puts on a helmet, no one can tell that a man or a woman is driving. Thanks to Janet Guthrie, the phrase became "Drivers, start your engines."

Janet Guthrie, the oldest of five children, was born in March 1938 in Iowa City, Iowa to Jean Ruth and William Lain Guthrie, both pilots. Her family moved to Miami, Florida when Janet was three years old after her father accepted a job with Eastern Airlines.

After graduating from the University of Michigan in 1960 with a degree in physics, Guthrie worked as a flight instructor and aerospace engineer in research and development for Republic Aviation, with the dream of becoming a scientist astronaut. When she didn't get the call from NASA (she didn't have a PhD), she decided on a new dream, auto racing.

Unlike her male racing counterparts at the time, Guthrie didn't have sponsorships or funding. She built her own engine, did her own bodywork and, to compete, she towed her Jaguar XK140 behind an old station wagon around the country. At night, she'd sleep in her car.

Guthrie accused the competitive racing industry on many occasions of racism and sexism. "The point is," she said, "there are no Blacks and no women in Indy car racing and stock car racing, and the reason is not an absence of talent."

Few women have repeated Guthrie's racing success. In 1977, she was the first woman to qualify and compete in the Indianapolis 500 and the Daytona 500. But, the lack of corporate sponsorships for female drivers was dismal to mostly none. "Sponsors want the publicity that racing brings," she protested. "Although a successful woman driver will get ten times the man's attention, it still comes back to the 'good old boy' network."

When Pippa Mann lacked the funding to enter the Indianapolis 500 in 2020, despite having driven in the previous year, the race was left with not a single woman driver. The struggle for women drivers to secure corporate sponsorships continues today.

Tennis legend Billie Jean King said of Guthrie: "The biggest difference between my challenge match with Bobby Riggs and Janet's historic races at Indianapolis and Daytona is the difference between hitting a ball into the net and hitting a concrete wall at 200 miles per hour. Janet put everything on the line, including her life."

Guthrie never sought attention because of her gender. She wanted to be judged solely on her qualifications behind the wheel. In 2006, she was inducted into the International Motorsports Hall of Fame. In 2019, she was inducted into the Automotive Hall of Fame (both for her achievements in motorsports). Guthrie's helmet and race suit are on display at the Smithsonian Institution as she was one of the first inductees in the International Women's Sports Hall of Fame. (She will not qualify for the NASCAR Hall of Fame because she didn't race for at least ten years.)

Janet Guthrie was married for 17 years to Warren Levine, a charter airline pilot. He died in 2006 of a sudden heart attack. Guthrie has lived in Aspen, Colorado for over 30 years, and is active in the town's art scene and several garden clubs. Her autobiography, *Janet Guthrie: A Life at Full Throttle,* is on Kindle.

PART SIX: BASEBALL

Women's barnstorming teams have always existed, and women have also played major league players in exhibition games. On April 2, 1931, 17-year-old Jackie Mitchell of the Chattanooga Lookouts struck out Babe Ruth *and* Lou Gehrig in an exhibition game. Embarrassed Commissioner of Baseball, Kennesaw Mountain Landis, voided her contract as a result.

Babe Ruth, the "Sultan of Swat," and owner of other idiotic monikers, once said of women ballplayers, "I don't know what's going to happen if they begin to let women in baseball. Of course, they will never make good. Why? Because they are too delicate. It would kill them to play ball every day."

Mary Elizabeth "Lizzie" Murphy was born April 13, 1894, in Warren, Rhode Island to working-class parents Mary and John Murphy. Although the younger Murphy loved baseball, she was also a runner, skater, and swimmer. If it was fast and exciting, she played it, much to her mother's dismay, who believed sports was unladylike. Her father encouraged his daughter's pursuits, thinking it was a passing phase. He was clearly wrong.

By age 12, Murphy had quit school, like other women, and gone to work at the Parker Woolen Mill. By age 15, she was playing on the local men's business amateur league teams. While baseball was her true love, Murphy was a born athlete. She participated in everything from ice hockey to soccer to swimming to long-distance running in her hometown during the early 1900s. She told a reporter once, in 1941, that she "always loved boys' sports. They're so active, and they wake you up." Her brother Henry claimed that no boy or girl could even come close to her on the ice.

When she began her professional baseball career, she was a pitcher but was also known as a hitter. It wasn't easy. Although she performed well at first base, she could not drown out the boos from the stands. Murphy made history in 1922 as the first female player to play against major league players in a National League All-Star game against the

Boston Braves. She was also the first woman to play in the Negro Leagues when she played first base for the Cleveland Colored Giants when they came through Rhode Island. One of her proudest moments was when she hit a single off the greatest pitcher in the Negro Leagues—Satchel Paige.

Unlike her male teammates who had their numbers sewn on their uniforms, Murphy had her name stitched on the front and back of her uniform so that the fans could easily recognize her. She was her own marketing department. She believed that she was who they came to see. Not only did she believe it, but eventually, so did her manager and the owner of the team.

The story goes that she did not get paid for a particular game even though all the males on the team did, so she held out in the next game knowing the fans were looking for the "girl with the strawberry-colored hair under her hat." The owner gave in, promising her not only a regular pay rate but also *a cut of the gate.*

Murphy played 17 seasons before retiring in 1935 at the age of 41. Her career batting average was .300. She married in her early forties, but only to have her husband die several years later. Because there was no money set aside and no pension, she returned to working at the woolen mill and cleaning houses to make a living.

Murphy died on July 27, 1964, at the age of 70. She was inducted into the Rhode Island Heritage Hall of Fame and honored in her hometown of Warren, Rhode Island, on her 100th anniversary in 1994.

"Laughable." "You gotta be kiddin'." "No way. Go home and fix your husband some biscuits." **Marcenia Lyle "Toni Tomboy" Stone** was born in 1921 in St. Paul, Minnesota. She was a member of the Negro American League's Indianapolis Clowns and was the first woman to ever play professional baseball as a regular on a big-league team. It didn't come easy. Stone was subjected to a barrage of insults from fans and sometimes even her teammates who objected to seeing a woman compete in a "men's" game. The complicated rules surrounding Jim Crow America only amplified the pressure as she and other Black players had to be careful not to patronize whites-only establishments.

Over the years, many people tried to dissuade the tomboy from playing ball, including her husband, but she hung in there. Most sports enthusiasts agree that had she been a man, she probably would have been promoted into the major leagues alongside Jackie Robinson. She was that good. All of these accomplishments may make her "one of the best players you have never heard of," according to the Negro League Baseball Players Association.

Her place was permanently cemented in modern baseball history when the Indianapolis Clowns of the Negro Leagues signed Stone to a pro contract to replace Hank Aaron, who left for the majors in 1953. She surprised most of the male players by becoming a more than competent second baseman. Her playing resume includes playing against Ernie Banks, Willie Mays, Buck O'Neil, and Jackie Robinson. And because the Indianapolis Clowns were to baseball what the Harlem Globetrotters were to basketball (combining athleticism, theater, and comedy in their style of play) Negro newspapers were not interested in reporting on "a girl ballplayer" on the Clowns.

No one, including her teammates, took her playing seriously. Her stats are still hard to find because Negro League teams kept poor statistics, if at all, and they indeed weren't maintaining statistics on a female.

Although she was part of the team, she was not allowed in the locker room. *Sometimes* she was allowed to change in the umpire's locker room. Even though she felt like she was "one of the guys," the players around her made it clear that she wasn't. They detested her presence. She was asked once to wear a skirt on the field, which made her almost sick at the thought. After a period with the Clowns, she was traded to the Kansas City Monarchs where she spent most of the season on the bench, next to the men who hated her. She called it hell.

Stone emerged from the pack of invisibility because she loved baseball, and many did not miss the fact that she was truly passionate about playing. She was inducted in 1993 into both the International Women's Sports Hall of Fame in Long Island, New York, and the Sudafed International Women's Sports Hall of Fame. Dunning Baseball Stadium in St. Paul, Minnesota, was renamed Toni Stone Field in 1996, and several theatrical plays around the country have been based on her life. In 2020, the Society for American Baseball Research nominated Stone for the **Dorothy Seymour Mills Lifetime Achievement Award.**

Stone met Aurelius Pescia Alberga, in a nightclub. She was 29, and he was 35 years her senior. They were married for 37 years until his death at age 103 in the late 1980s. Toni Stone died November 2, 1996, at age 75 of heart failure in Alameda, California.

During World War II, professional baseball players were not exempt from the draft. When most of the quality players left for war, the teams were left with marginal players, at best.

The All-American Girls Professional Baseball League (AAGPBL) began as a joke hatched by several Major League Baseball owners to keep baseball going, and their pockets lined while the men were at war.

It was suggested by the chewing gum king, Phillip K. Wrigley, that women could replace the men and play on the teams. Once the laughter died down, Wrigley et al. got to work and organized the AAGPBL. Surprisingly, but only to the men, they were able to find some very impressive female ballplayers, and at the height of its popularity (1948-50), the League had teams in 12 cities. One of the most successful teams was the Rockford Peaches from Illinois, which won four championships.

The female players were heckled from every angle of the field, but because they were passionate about playing, most could drown out the hurtful noise. The majority of the "skilled and attractive" women hailed from rural areas of the United States. The AAGPBL remained unofficially segregated, claiming that only white women met their exacting beauty standards. Albeit there was an abundance of women of color who could play ball, they were not encouraged to try out for the teams. It wasn't *all* due to racism from the managers. Some rationale pointed to the various towns the girls would be playing in, and safety would be a significant factor facing women of color.

The AAGPBL started with four clubs in 1943 and before folding in 1954, and for most of the League's history, manager Bill Allington coached several teams and led the League in career wins as a manager.

Jean Faut, the second oldest of six children, was born in East Greenville, Pennsylvania, in 1925 to working-class parents. Considered the greatest overhand pitcher of the AAGPBL, the sandy-haired, blue-eyed, and attractive Faut developed a love for all sports, but especially baseball. She got her start at third base as a youngster but was soon taught how to throw various pitches by a high school friend. She found she loved pitching.

The year she graduated from high school World War II was still raging, so like other young women her age Faut went to work in a factory. She played ball as often as she could. An AAGPBL scout from nearby Allentown was looking for female ballplayers and liked what he saw in Faut. So, with encouragement from family and friends, Faut decided to chance it and try out for the All-American League spring training camp in Pascagoula, Mississippi. She felt that the all-day bus ride was less punishing than the several days of calisthenics, drills, and practices, but Faut made the League and was picked up as a pitcher for the South Bend (Indiana) Blue Sox.

Faut enjoyed her rookie season with South Bend even though they took third place. As a right-handed pitcher and an unbelievable third baseman, she quickly became a four-time All-Star and a two-time Player of the Year. She also became the highest-paid Blue Sox star in the late 1940s (probably making more than her father). Her remarkable achievements in eight seasons with South Bend included pitching *four no-hitters* and wait for it...*two perfect games*!

Most girls who played in the AAGPBL were single, which allowed them to travel, go on un-chaperoned dates, and, most importantly, not have to report their whereabouts to men, something their mothers never envisioned. In late 1947 Faut married a former minor league pitcher named Karl Winsch, who hailed from her hometown of East Greenville. They settled in South Bend, where Faut worked off-season for US Rubber Company. She immediately became pregnant. She now had to balance housekeeping, a husband, a job, and a baby, but she wasn't going to let anything stop her from playing baseball. Although she missed the 1948 spring training camp, she was still able to rank seventh among pitchers hurling 45 or more innings. In 1949 Faut became the best measurement of herself by assembling a 24-8 record with a 1.10 ERA. She alone led the

League in one category: 12 shutouts.

In 1952, the Blue Sox hired Faut's husband as the manager, who became increasingly harsh in his treatment of the players. Before the end of the season, the players wouldn't speak to him or Faut, who was caught in the middle. Winsch's respectability factor hit an all-time low when he suspended a player who responded not as quickly as he would have liked to pinch-run late in a game. Six players had had enough and walked out. Somehow, the team still made the playoffs.

In Faut's final season in 1953, she was once again voted Player of the Year even though the Blue Sox missed the post-season play. After the AAGPBL disbanded in 1954, Faut, still laced with a competitive drive, began bowling and turned professional in 1960. She then bowled for several years on the women's pro tour. In 1968 at the age of 43, she divorced Karl Winsch.

Faut married again in 1977 to Charles Eastman, a resident of Rock Hill, South Carolina. They were married for 26 years until his death in 2003. At the tender age of 95, Jean Faut, the mother of two and grandmother of four, currently resides in Rock Hill, South Carolina. She was inducted into the National Women's Baseball Hall of Fame in 2012.

PART SEVEN: BASKETBALL

In girls' basketball at the end of the nineteenth century, there were special rules for girls: you could only hold the ball for three-seconds and only dribble three times before passing the ball. Laughable now.

It was a great moment in the early years of women's basketball when "bloomers" were introduced at Sophie Newcomb College in New Orleans by Clara Gregory Baer in 1896. This move toward wearing functional clothing was probably due to women players shouting, "Enough already with the floor-length dresses, especially on the basketball court!" Most of these players tripped over their hems while playing, and not surprisingly, most of them ended up with broken bones and black eyes.

In those same first days of basketball, female players would post guards at the gymnasium doors and windows to keep the men from watching them. Boy, have times changed. Today women *wish* the men would pay attention to their game (financially speaking) as they have become incredible athletes.

There are only minor differences today between women's basketball and men's basketball. The ball is smaller, and the three-point line is closer, and the women's game is not played above the rim. Some of today's WNBA players can probably play as well as the men. And for many basketball purists, the women's game is a more accurate reflection of how the game is supposed to be played. Okay, so the women play closer to the ground and don't dunk as often as men, but this may even be a good thing.

In the beginning, women basketball players were "encouraged" to wear makeup and lipstick to the games to submerge any idea they might be lesbians. Because, you know, according to the then press, "It's not natural to be an athlete and a heterosexual woman at the same time."

Even today, some women athletes have surrendered to this idea.

Senda Berenson was the second of five children born to Albert and Judith Valvrojenski in March 1868. Her parents were Lithuanian Jews who would emigrate to the US when she was seven years old. Prior to their move, Albert became a practitioner of Haskalah, a European movement that advocated more integration of Jews into secular society.

Some folks didn't care for Albert's rhetoric. After his home and lumber business was burned to the ground, Albert decided to move to the US to raise his family according to his own beliefs. The family settled in a Boston section with almost 50 families from their original neighborhood, some of whom were relatives. Albert then changed his surname to Berenson soon after his arrival as part of his "Westernization."

Senda Berenson was a sickly and weak child who never indulged in anything athletic. She was so weak she couldn't even play the piano as it took too much energy. She was home-schooled and taught reading and languages by her father. To improve her strength and stamina, she was encouraged to attend the Boston Normal School of Gymnastics.

At first, she couldn't get with the action plan, but then she committed to the idea of getting healthy and finished the program two years later. She learned anatomy, physiology, and hygiene so completely that she was qualified to teach gymnastics. Without a high school diploma or college degree, Berenson, at age 23, began teaching physical education at Smith College.

Of course, in 1891, the atmosphere toward women athletes was not at all flattering. So, to say that females flocked to her class would be uh...lying. But Berenson believed so much in exercising and good health that she would not let this inaction shake her beliefs. She had to look for an alternative to get girls and women into physical education.

She then heard about a new game called "basket ball" invented by James Naismith, a teacher, who during a harsh New England winter, found that the boys confined inside school were becoming unruly. He believed they needed an indoor distraction to keep them out of trouble, and give them something to do.

Group games were not the norm at Smith College, but Berenson felt this would be an exciting experiment, mainly because women had never played in group games before. Yes, they rowed, fenced, and conditioned themselves to archery and horseback riding but those were mostly singular-type activities.

After meeting Dr. Naismith at a conference and receiving his encouragement to adopt the sport as a team exercise for her female students, Berenson got to work. Known as the "Mother of Women's Basketball," Berenson was the first to introduce and adopt rules for women's "basket ball" to Smith College in 1899, modifying the existing men's rules.

She then wrote and developed the official rule book for women's collegiate "basket ball" and numerous articles on the new sport. The first official publication of its kind, *Basket Ball for Women*, was published by the Spalding Athletic Library in 1901, with Berenson as its editor. Many of the rules developed for women were used for more than 70 years.

In 1911, at the age of 43, Berenson married Herbert Vaughn Abbott, an English professor at Smith College. She resigned her post at Smith and became the director of physical education at a private girls' school until 1921. Berenson died in Santa Barbara, California, on February 16, 1954, at the age of 86. Her contributions to basketball were recognized when she became the first woman enshrined in the Naismith Memorial Basketball Hall of Fame in 1985.

Nera D. White was born on November 15, 1935, the eldest of seven children born to Horace White, a teacher, coach, and farmer, and the former Lois Birdean Fishburn White. The younger White grew up on a farm just outside of Lafayette, Tennessee. She was expected to help with farm chores daily and also helped raise her younger siblings. White was a 1954 graduate of Macon County High School, where her sports career began.

As a freshman, White was a starting player on the high school girls' basketball team and was voted the most valuable player for her high school district in 1954. After graduating from Macon, White attended George Peabody College for Teachers in Nashville, now part of Vanderbilt University, for four years. Peabody did not have a women's basketball team, so White started playing on an AAU team sponsored by Nashville Business College. She led her team to ten national championships, was named MVP of the AAU National Tournament nine times, and was named AAU All-American fifteen years in a row.

Playing when a professional women's basketball league in the US was considered a joke, White distinguished herself, receiving many honors as one of the greatest female players in history. In 1957-58, she led the US to the World Basketball Championship in Rio de Janeiro, where she earned another MVP honor.

White was "widely acknowledged as the greatest woman ever to play the game of basketball." In 1957, she led the US national women's basketball team to win the World Championship against Russia. Afterward, she was named MVP of the tournament and was named the Best Woman Player in the World. Throughout White's career, she received numerous awards, including her induction to the Naismith Memorial Basketball Hall of Fame and the Women's Basketball Hall of Fame.

She was not only talented in basketball; she was an astonishing softball player too.

But a professional basketball career was not in the cards for White who retired from basketball at the age of 33 in 1969. There was no pension. There was no money set aside for her "old" age, noting that basketball "had given her two bad knees and had not provided for her economically. It had only given her some dusty trophies and worthless certificates." She continued to work at a print shop until she was laid off after the owner's death in 1982. She was only 47 years old. After that, she moved back to her family farm in Lafayette.

White's high school gym in her hometown of Lafayette is named after her, and the local highway (State Route 10 north) was renamed Nera White Highway. White was one of the pioneers of women's basketball, and most sportswriters concur that, "She probably did not get her due because she was a woman and women in athletics weren't looked up to in her day like they are now."

"Did I have game?" Nera White once remarked. "You know that move [Michael] Jordan made on the Lakers, switching the ball from one hand to the other? I was doing that in the '50s."

Nera White died on April 13, 2016, at the age of 80. She is survived by a son, Jeff, and three granddaughters.

Lusia Harris was born February 10, 1955, in Minter City, Mississippi to Ethel and Willie Harris, cranberry farmers. She is the tenth of eleven children, and all of her brothers and one of her sisters also played basketball. Harris won the most valuable player award three consecutive years in high school. She planned to attend Alcorn State University, which graduated her hero, civil rights icon Medgar Evers, but it did not have a women's basketball team. However, in Cleveland, Mississippi, Delta State University started a collegiate women's team, so she jumped at the offer to attend. This was all before Title IX, so Delta State offered no sports scholarships for women.

Harris attended Delta State on a combination of academic scholarships and work-study funds. She was selected to represent the US in the 1976 Summer Olympics in Montreal, Canada, the first women's basketball tournament in the

Olympic Games. She scored the first-ever points in women's Olympic basketball. The US team won three games and lost two games to Japan and the Soviet Union, who went undefeated and won the gold medal, while the US brought home the silver. Harris played in all five games, averaging 15.2 points and 7.0 rebounds per game.

In the seventh round of the 1970 NBA Draft, the New Orleans Jazz selected Harris with the 137th pick. She became the second woman ever drafted by an NBA team after Denise Long, chosen by the San Francisco Warriors in the 1969 Draft. However, the league voided the Warriors' selection; thus, Harris became the first and only woman ever officially drafted. Harris did not express an interest in playing in the NBA and declined to try out for the Jazz because, unbeknownst to everyone, she was pregnant, which made it physically impossible for her to attend the Jazz training camp. But she was selected ahead of 33 male players. In a poll on the NBA website, Harris was ranked as the most unusual pick in the NBA draft history.

Harris was inducted in the Delta State's Hall of Fame in 1983. In 1992, Harris and former player Nera White became the first two women players inducted into the Naismith Memorial Basketball Hall of Fame. In 1999, Harris and her Delta State coach, Margaret

Wade, and her teammates Nancy Lieberman, Ann Meyers, and Pat Head, were among the 26 inaugural inductees to the Women's Basketball Hall of Fame. Harris was also named to the International Women's Sports Hall of Fame.

Harris married George E. Stewart on February 4, 1977. They have two sons and twin daughters.

PART EIGHT: THOROUGHBRED RACING

Why is it that a governing body only listens when they're being sued?

In 1968, a handful of women, undeservedly called "jockettes" by a short-sighted press, had begun demanding the right to apply for jockey licenses, citing the Civil Rights Act of 1964, which banned discrimination in hiring based on race, religion, sex, or national origin. The majority of their applications were rejected by racing's red tape division, which alleged that women were unqualified to participate due to "physical limitations" and "emotional instability." Female jockeys who attempted to ride met with boycotts by male jockeys.

In 1968, US Olympic equestrian Kathy Kusner became the first licensed female jockey after she sued the Maryland Racing Commission for denying her application for a jockey's license based on gender. In the same year, Penny Ann Early was granted a jockey license, but she was refused three times to race when male jockeys boycotted the race to compete. The sexism and chauvinism stench from the horse tracks didn't all come from the jockeys, especially since it is the horse's trainer who chooses jockeys, and unfortunately and usually, all the trainers are men. So, at this writing, this statistic still stands.

Over the years, there have just been six (total) women jockeys who have competed in professional racing. Only 10 percent of jockeys are women. The closest any woman has ever come to winning was in 2013 when Rosie Napravnik came in fifth place. And while she never won the Kentucky Derby, Napravnik did win the Louisiana Derby and the Kentucky Oaks.

But let's back up. First, there was Diane Crump.

Diane Crump was born in 1948 in Milford, Connecticut, the daughter of Walter and Jean Crump. While still a youngster, her family moved to Florida to buy a piece of property to build a marina. The wheels started turning in the younger Crump's head, as she formulated a plan. "My parents promised me when we moved to Florida I would get a horse," she said, adding that she also took any odd job she could find to aid in the purchase of such animal. "I delivered newspapers and mowed lawns. When I turned 12, I had saved up $150." She later began taking riding lessons at age 13.

As a teenager, Crump galloped horses in both Kentucky and Florida. She purchased her first pony from a newspaper ad, and the seller taught her basic horsemanship and how to trail ride. Once the Crump family found the property they liked, the seller offered an interesting proposition. If father Crump bought the land the seller would throw in the two mares on the property. As the story goes, father Crump bought the land.

In the winter of 1969, in the wake of the Kathy Kusner decision, Diane Crump broke through the gates of what had been a men's-only club on February 7, 1969, when she received a jockey's license at Hialeah after showing the stewards that she could handle a horse out of the gate.

From that point on, she would receive endless left-handed compliments from some of the jockeys who rode against her. But there was no mistaking the position of Nick Jemas, who at that time headed the Jockeys' Guild. "There are 82 good reasons why men and women shouldn't ride against each other," Jemas said. "There have been 82 jockeys killed in racing accidents since 1940."

Heeding his warning but not allowing it to dictate her future, Diane Crump became the first woman to compete as a professional jockey in the Kentucky Derby. She sat atop a three-year-old named Fathom who was just a miler and didn't belong in the Derby, but whose owner, whiskey baron W. L. Lyons Brown, was up there in age, on his last legs, and had nothing better to do with his money. He took her on because he "wanted to dance just once." Men with money—happens all the time in the Kentucky Derby. Sometimes these owners have won, almost by accident.

There was so much hostility toward Crump just because she was a female that she required a police escort to get to the track, taking her through an angry crowd of shouting people. The hecklers were yelling at her to "Go back to the kitchen and cook dinner." She believed the hecklers thought she was going to be the downfall of the whole sport.

She had ridden a 48-1 shot to a 10th-place finish in a 12-horse race at Hialeah, becoming the first female jockey to compete at a pari-mutuel track. (A betting system in which all bets of a particular type are placed together in a pool, then taxes and the "house-take" are deducted, and payoff odds are calculated by sharing the pool among all winning bets.)

She didn't win that day, but at the age of 20, Crump looked forward to the exciting years that lay ahead. It was not easy, as in the previous year, two women were forced out of horse races they had entered after male jockeys threw rocks at the trailers used as locker rooms by the women and threatened a boycott. Crump was only permitted to compete when officials threatened to fine the male jockeys who were boycotting the races she entered.

On February 1, 1989, at the age of 41, Crump suffered a broken leg, ankle, and ribs from a riding accident and was hospitalized for ten days. Her leg was broken in multiple places, and doctors told her she would never be able to ride again. After this injury, Crump decided to hang up the idea of racing and work as a trainer for a small stable at the Middleburg Training Center in Virginia.

Crump finally retired from racing in 1999. She and her horse trainer husband Don Divine now run an equine sales business and live in

Virginia. In 2020, a biography, *Diane Crump: A Horse Racing Pioneer's Life in the Saddle* by Mark Shrager, was published by Lyons Press.

PART NINE: AMERICAN BILLIARDS

Minnesota Fats, Fast Eddie, The Miz, Mr. Pocket Billiards, Detroit Whitey, The Baltimore Kid, and of course "Wimpy" couldn't be left out of the fray when it comes to billiard players and their nicknames.

Women didn't need labels in billiards because they were able to etch their real names in stone for all to see, like Jean Balukas, Ewa Mataya Laurance, Allison Fisher, Jeanette Lee, et al., all made credible because of Dorothy Wise.

Dorothy Wise was born in Spokane, Washington, in 1914, at the beginning of World War I in Europe. When she first started playing pool professionally, there were few to nil national tournaments for women. Dorothy learned to play pool from her husband, Jimmy Wise, who managed billiard parlors in several cities in the western part of the US. She credits Jimmy for her high-level skill in playing.

When women took the sport of billiards seriously, Dorothy began winning numerous local and state tournaments. The first national tournament for women happened in 1967. Although her husband was able to watch her win the first national championship, he, unfortunately, died later that year. Not to let her husband down, Dorothy kept winning for the next five years, losing the title in 1972 to a 13-year-old prodigy named Jean Balukas.

Dorothy became a member of the Billiard Congress of America Hall of Fame in 1981. She was also the first woman to be made a member. Dorothy never had children and never remarried. She died at age 81 in 1995.

Jean Balukas was a child prodigy in the game of billiards. She was born in Brooklyn, New York on June 28, 1959, to parents who already had four boys. Although not billiards players themselves, her parents purchased a pool table for their basement to keep their four teenage boys out of the poolrooms. They never once believed their daughter would become the pool shark.

Balukas entered the public's attention at six years old during a pool exhibition held at New York City's Grand Central Terminal. Shortly thereafter, she appeared on various television shows including a popular program called *I've Got a Secret*. She placed fifth in the 1969 US Open straight pool championship and placed fourth and third respectively in the following two US Opens—and she was only nine years old! From that early start, Balukas completely dominated women's professional pool throughout the 1970s and 80s.

Most folks described Balukas as a "…trailblazer, a loner who rebelled against dress codes for women…" Regardless of the monikers, she is a five-time **Billiards Congress of America (BCA) Player of the Year, the youngest inductee into the BCA Hall of Fame,** and the second woman given the honor (after Dorothy Wise), and was ranked fifteenth on Billiard Digest's Fifty Greatest Players of the twentieth century.

Balukas won the US Open from 1972 through 1978, accumulating six world championship titles and over 100 professional competition first-place finishes with 38 majors to her name. She then went on to enjoy a streak of 16 first-place finishes in women's professional tournaments. And was the only woman to compete on equal footing with men in professional play during her ascent. She courageously quit playing in 1988 while at the height of her career because of a dispute.

According to a 1987 interview with the *New York Times,* "[Balukas] learned that, even in fun, pool stars did not like losing in public, especially not to children, but most especially, not to girls." She also discovered that young men, including her brothers, shared the feeling of shame over losing to girls.

The story goes that Balukas was slated for competition in New York in both the men's and women's divisions. After arriving, she discovered that she would be required to wear formal attire for evening-scheduled matches, attire that she did not bring. The men's division, she learned, had no similar dress code. Balukas voiced that women should not be treated differently from men, and therefore refused to purchase clothing just to meet unfair sanctions.

Ironically, it was the women players who voted Balukas out of the tournament. She later said that "what hurt most was that while I was trying to stand up for us being treated the same as men, the other girls held the tournament draw without me. By one vote, they kept me out. And some of the girls who (were) my best friends voted against me."

According to the Women's Professional Billiards Association (WPBA), "The dress code was self-imposed by the players in an attempt to improve the image of women's pool and to attract more spectators and press to the sport, and that Balukas was the only participant...unwilling to comply."

Balukas refused to believe that her professional rivals had their self-interest at stake, and that they would have a much better chance at the $5,000 first-place prize award with her out of the competition. Not long afterward, she felt it was time to leave the game she loved and indicated to a reporter that she was "thinking of dropping out of women's competition altogether."

After retiring from professional billiards, Balukas returned to her hometown of Brooklyn and took over her father's billiard hall. Her family quickly changed Ovington Billiards' name to Hall of Fame Billiards in recognition of Balukas's celebrity. The *New York Times* described Balukas's dominance over women's professional pool as "breathtaking."

Balukas, now 62, is concentrating on another game with a ball and a hole–golf. She is also staying in her beloved Brooklyn.

PART TEN: ICE HOCKEY

Manon Rhéaume was born on February 24, 1972, in Quebec, Canada, to athletic parents. Growing up, playing hockey with her brothers and the boys in the area, Rhéaume learned pretty quickly that, despite her abilities, she was often cut from teams simply because she was a girl. Although it was frustrating, she persevered and continued to work hard and hone her skills to prove she could compete with the boys. "So many times when I was younger," she said, "I was good enough to make the top level. I was good enough to be on the team, but they didn't want me because I was a girl."

When she turned 12, she became the first girl to play in the famed Quebec International Pee-Wee Hockey Tournament. Seven years later, she made history again, becoming the first woman to play in the Quebec Major Junior Hockey League. Rhéaume also represented Canada in international women's hockey. She was part of the World Championship women's team in 1992 and 1994 and helped Team Canada win the Olympic silver medal in 1998, the first year that women's hockey was included in the Olympic Winter Games.

Rhéaume had been invited to the Tampa Bay (Florida) Lightning team's training camp after a Lightning scout spotted her playing. The Lightning's then-general manager, Phil Esposito, one of the greatest hockey players in NHL history, watched her play but thought she was a small guy. He was stunningly surprised to find she was a girl. Esposito liked her skills as a goalie and immediately decided this could be a way to get Floridians excited about hockey, especially since Florida folks knew nothing about ice hockey!

Rhéaume didn't care if this was a publicity stunt for the new expansion team; it was her chance to be on a professional hockey team as a player! "When I was younger, so many times people said no to me to play at a higher level because I was a girl. So, this time around, if they said yes to me because I (am) a girl, I'm taking this opportunity."

She was unbelievably nervous as she stepped out onto the ice against the St. Louis Blues on September 23, 1992. But once she got on the ice, she was calm. She was playing hockey, a game she knew all too well. As the goalie she faced nine shots, and only two went in. Although being on the ice as a professional was truly nerve-racking, she knew her performance was important. But it was more than important; it was historic.

Although it was 28 years ago, Rhéaume didn't understand at the time her momentous turn on the ice and the decades of inspiration that would follow. "Back then, I didn't realize the impact I would have on young girls or people in general or even boys that play hockey," she said. "Later in life, having parents come up to me and say, 'You're such an inspiration for my daughters.' Even still today, young kids are doing projects on me at school because they read about me. They were not even born. That's when I realized what I did had a positive impact on people."

She closed a lot of mouths. "A lot of people thought one woman wouldn't be there," she said. "Hopefully, they are proved wrong again."

Rhéaume was married briefly in 1998 to Gerry St. Cyr, a minor league hockey player; the union produced a son, Dylan. She later married again producing another son, Dokada. In 2000, Rhéaume joined Mission

Hockey in Irvine, California, as director of global marketing for women's hockey. In her three years with the company, she helped develop the first women-specific hockey products. In 2008, she established the Manon Rhéaume Foundation, which provides scholarships to girls under 19 to help them pursue their athletic dreams.

PART ELEVEN: CEILING BREAKERS

Women, regardless of their race, are to this writing rare as baseball executives. The year 2020 was, for the most part, taxing, strange, horrible, fantastic, but primarily illuminating. Kudos to Kim Ng because she is the first woman to become a Major League Baseball General Manager. She is also the first woman hired as a GM by any major professional men's team in North American sports.

However, 85 years ago, it was **Effa Louise Manley.** She was part-owner of the Newark Eagles, a championship Negro League baseball team that produced eight future MLB Hall of Famers: Leon Day, Ray Dandridge, Larry Doby, Monte Irvin, Biz Mackey, Don

Newcombe, Mule Suttles, and Effa herself, the first female executive in baseball who thrived in an industry overwhelmingly run by men.

Effa Brooks was born March 27, 1900, in Philadelphia to a white mother and a wealthy white man her mother had an affair with while married, with children, to a Black man. (Still with me?) Although Effa looked different from her half-brothers and sisters, her mother didn't tell her she was white until she was almost a grown woman. Effa never told anyone that she was white until she was in her seventies. Why? She had a Black stepfather, Black half-siblings, lived in a Black neighborhood, married a Black man, was a civil rights advocate. As far as she was concerned, she was Black. And no one ever took time to argue the point.

Effa met her future husband, Abe Manley, at the 1932 World Series in Yankee Stadium. He was wealthy from a few nefarious dealings and 15 years her senior. Although the thunderbolt struck Abe, he did not recognize immediately that his soon-to-be wife was a trailblazer who would help him turn a dismal Brooklyn Eagles baseball team into the championship Newark Eagles. Nine months after their initial encounter, it would become the second marriage for both.

Although Effa attended quite a few baseball games, mostly because she was crazy about Babe Ruth, she wasn't really into baseball until she met Abe, a baseball fanatic. When he purchased the Brooklyn Eagles, he changed the name, hired new managers, sought out the best players, and negotiated their salaries. Effa then became the administration part of the operation:

- Handling promotions and travel schedules.
- Getting contracts signed.
- Reviewing schedules.
- Making uniforms available and clean for every game.
- Accepting IOUs.
- Granting advances (especially when a player could not afford to return to Newark from off-season).
- Making sure that the equipment was in good playing condition.

Effa never shrank from mixing it up with the good ol' boy establishment. She was progressive and aggressive and did not allow the male power structure that ran baseball to go unchallenged. Of course, the power structure did not feel comfortable with her in the room, and Effa would, at these times, shake her head in exasperation. Several times other owners would politely ask Abe to leave his wife at home. He ignored them. She was a thorn in their side—Abe knew it, and so did she. But Abe thought Effa's often suggestions (perhaps not her delivery) regarding keeping tighter and concise statistics were "spot on."

When World War II ended, MLB became interested in a revenue stream stemming from an overlooked demographic—Negro fans. Integration was the answer, and Effa was right on the mark. She believed when MLB finally opened up to men of color, the organizations stealing these players should pay compensation to the Negro League organization from which they were stealing. She was the Negro Leagues' champion for team compensation once players began jumping to the MLB.

This idea didn't catch on quickly with the Negro League owners (duh), but it did catch the attention of Bill Veeck and Branch Rickey, MLB Executives who probably wished she would lower the volume of her rhetoric. Syd Pollock, the Indianapolis Clowns' owner, was one of the few Negro League team owners who managed to receive compensation for the players he sold to the major leagues. Effa wanted MLB executives to understand clearly that the Negro League contained a collection of top-notch Black ballplayers who could equal or eclipse the pitching, throwing, and fielding ability of any white player...any day, any time.

Abe and Effa sold the Eagles to investors in 1946, two years before the Leagues folded completely. They were able to salvage most of their investment once the Negro Leagues folded. Other owners, not so much or not at all. When Abe died in 1952, Effa moved to California to be near family.

Following her ownership tenure, Effa co-authored a book on Black baseball and donated her scrapbook, chronicling her time as an owner, to the National Baseball Hall of Fame. She also presented letters in which she lobbied for Negro Leaguers to be admitted into Cooperstown. Effa never had children. By the spring of 1981, her health had deteriorated to the point that she could no longer live alone in her apartment. She moved into a rest home run by former Negro League player Quincy Troupe. A month later, colon cancer had emerged big time, which progressed into peritonitis post-surgery. Effa died after suffering a heart attack on April 16, 1981, at the age of 80 years old, four days after the death of her sports idol, boxer Joe Louis.

Helen Bates "Penny" Chenery was born January 27, 1922, into an affluent family in New Rochelle, New York. The youngest of three children, she was named for her mother. Her father Christopher, emerged from scratch-poor beginnings to found two utility companies in Virginia, and then later, because he loved horses, established a thoroughbred racing and horse breeding operation.

Young Chenery attended prestigious preparatory schools before graduating from Smith College. She then attended Columbia Business School, where she was one of only 20 women in a class of 800 men. She met her future husband, John "Jack" Tweedy, at Columbia. At her parents' almost insistence, she dropped out of school only a few months shy of receiving her MBA to marry Jack. They moved to Denver, Colorado, where Tweedy was a group member that founded Vail Ski Resort in the early 1960s. He later became Chairman of the Board of Vail Associates.

In 1969 Chenery's life changed forever when her mother died suddenly, and her father suffered a stroke. He remained in the hospital in New Rochelle for several years until his death. Chenery's two siblings wanted to sell the horse operation because they felt the farm had been sorely neglected and was no longer profitable. But Penny couldn't bear the thought of abandoning her father's dream of producing a winning horse. So, she got to work.

First, she had to talk her husband into letting her return to the farm in Virginia to peruse the assets and liabilities. Second, she had to explain to her four children the importance of her being away for a while. Third, after months of cutting costs by scaling back on equipment and employees, she also had to fire their top trainer Casey Hayes, who she believed was skimming money from the Meadow Farm amid conflict-of-interest schemes.

Lastly, she had to hire Roger Laurin to train and manage the stables. After Laurin departed several months later to work for the Phipps Family Stables (a more prestigious operation), he sent his father Lucien to take his place at Meadow Stable. With Lucien's help, the Meadow Farm produced Riva Ridge, a horse that brought in over $500,000 in purses in late 1971. This financial gain made it possible for Meadow Stable to get back on its feet. Riva Ridge then went on to win the 1972 Kentucky Derby and the Belmont Stakes, losing out at the Preakness.

Also housed in the Meadow's stable was two-year-old Secretariat, who became American Horse of the Year in late 1972 (a rare honor for a two-year-old), which solidified in Chenery the idea that Secretariat was going to be her father's dream horse.

Christopher Chenery died in January 1973, and the farm owed such a large tax bill that Penny had to rely on her "almost" MBA background to save the farm (again). But to keep the farm, she felt she had no other option but to syndicate Secretariat's breeding rights.

Chenery believed in every fiber of her body that Secretariat would win the three premier races in 1973: Kentucky Derby, Preakness, and Belmont Stakes. No one believed it; no one, and she had to convince a horde of men that Secretariat was what they should be betting on...starting with her husband, who did not have her back, but neither did her sister nor her brother.

In addition to battling the good old boys in the horse racing establishment, Chenery was also doing battle at home. She was constantly flying back and forth from Doswell, Virginia to her family home in Denver, Colorado. She was still handling the laundry, cooking meals, and making sure the four kids were still somewhat emotionally stable. She was even helping with homework. But she and Jack were now pretending to be a couple, and many women bashed Chenery for not putting her family above business.

These particular women missed the point. Jack Tweedy was a very wealthy lawyer, and he could have moved his practice east for any length of time so that his wife could care for her ailing father and take care of the farm operation without the added burden of her being jet-lagged every week. He could have shown his children, especially his sons, what supporting a wife on a mission looked like. But not Tweedy. He believed she, not he, should be taking care of the kids instead of trying to save a farm from a bygone era.

To garner the necessary funds for the syndication of Secretariat, Chenery needed to talk to someone who was considered a leader in the horse racing establishment. That person would be Ogden Phipps, the shopping mall's creator, who owned the prestigious Phipps Family Stables. After almost guaranteeing Phipps that Secretariat would take home the Triple Crown, Phipps must have believed in her because he agreed to the syndication, and shortly after that, all the other necessary owners and breeders fell in line. Now all she had to do was talk Secretariat into winning the three races.

Exercise riders, grooms, and stablemates at the Meadow all concurred that Penny Chenery and Secretariat shared a special bond. In 1973, Secretariat became the first Triple Crown winner in 25 years, setting records that still stand in all three races and winning the Belmont Stakes by an unheard-of 31 lengths.

In 1976, Chenery served for eight years as President of the Thoroughbred Owners and Breeders Association. In 1983, Penny Chenery, Martha F. Gerry, and Allaire DuPont became the first women admitted in the all-male Jockey Club. In 2003, the Arlington Park Track outside Chicago established the annual "Penny Chenery Distinguished Woman in Racing Award." In 2006, the National

Thoroughbred Racing Association honored her with the "Eclipse Award of Merit" for a lifetime of outstanding achievement in thoroughbred racing. In 2018, the National Museum of Racing and Hall of Fame named Penny Chenery a "Pillar of the Turf," the highest honor given to owners and breeders of Thoroughbreds. Both horses, Secretariat and Riva Ridge, were inducted into the National Museum of Racing and Hall of Fame. Chenery also strove to promote research into the dreaded disease of laminitis, the cause of Secretariat's death, and for a ban on performance-enhancing drugs in racing.

Chenery divorced Jack Tweedy after Secretariat's historic win. She remarried briefly a couple of years later to a long-time friend, but it didn't work out and, after divorcing, moved back to Colorado to be near her children and grandchildren. Penny Chenery died in September 2017, at the tender age of 95.

Phyllis Ann George was born on June 25, 1949, in Denton, Texas, 40 miles south of Dallas; an area where "the grasses of the prairies are the most conspicuous offerings of vegetation from mother nature." Her father, Robert, owned an oil distributorship. Her mother, Diantha Louise (Cogdell) George, was a homemaker. George attended North Texas

State University for three years until she was crowned Miss Texas in 1970. At that time, Texas Christian University awarded scholarships to Miss Texas honorees, so George had no problem adding 51 miles to her commute to TCU. She dropped out only because she won the Miss America crown later that fall.

George had high hopes of becoming a classical pianist, especially after taking piano lessons for more than a decade. But a career of tickling the ivories was not in the cards. The closest she ever came to playing piano in front of a large audience was when she played "Raindrops Keep Falling on My Head" as part of the talent portion of the Miss America Pageant...which she won.

In the early 70s, CBS Sports wanted to hire a woman who would provide a human interest angle that male commentators did not seem to want to do. George was warm, attractive, and knew sports...sorta. What she brought to the sports viewing table was young women and...men.

In 1975, she broke the glass ceiling in men's sportscasting as she became known for her interviews with athletes. She was one of the high-profile stars on CBS's "The NFL Today," the nation's premier pre-game football show. It was an awe-inspiring role for a woman.

But it wasn't all peaches and cream because, when she first got started, she received so much hate mail because she was a woman in a man's arena that she almost quit...almost. She persevered because she learned to cherish only the positive messages and mail.

George went on to host a talk show on the Nashville Network, write books and start two businesses: "Chicken by George," a maker of marinated fresh chicken breast entrees, which she sold to Hormel, and produced a line of cosmetics and skincare products called "Phyllis George Beauty," marketed through Home Shopping Network.

At age 35, George was diagnosed with a rare blood cancer called polycythemia rubra vera. Thirty-five years later, on May 14, 2020, this cancer would take her life. She was 70 years old. She is survived by a daughter Pamela, and son, Lincoln, and two grandchildren. Her marriages to Virginia Governor John Brown and Hollywood Producer Robert Evans both ended in divorce. Leslie Visser, a Sports Lifetime Achievement Winner and first female NFL analyst on both radio and TV, said of Phyllis George's passing, "For women in this (sports) business, we have lost a gentle giant."

Image credits courtesy of Pixabay

Swimming
Image by Gerd Altmann from Pixabay

Golf
Image by Ludek Domabyl from Pixabay

Track and Field
Image by Ray Shrewsberry • Thanks for
Downloads and Likes from Pixabay

Tennis
Image by efes from Pixabay

Baseball
Image by Felikss Veilands from Pixabay

Race Car Driving
Image by Robert Chalmers from Pixabay

Basketball
Image by Clker-Free-Vector-Images from Pixabay

Thoroughbred Racing
Image by Gorkhs from Pixabay

Billiards
Image by mwagner1 from Pixabay

Ice Hockey
Image by soerli from Pixabay

Breaking the glass ceiling
iStock photo, by mj0007

Gender Equality in Sport logo from clipartmax

JoAnn Fastoff is an award-winning author of both fiction and non-fiction books, including *White Sox (and other baseball worth mentioning) for Women.*

www.JoAnnFastoff.com

Printed by Libri Plureos GmbH in Hamburg, Germany